SCREW CHOCOLATE

YYC QUEEER WRITERS

CURATED BY M. JANE COLETTE

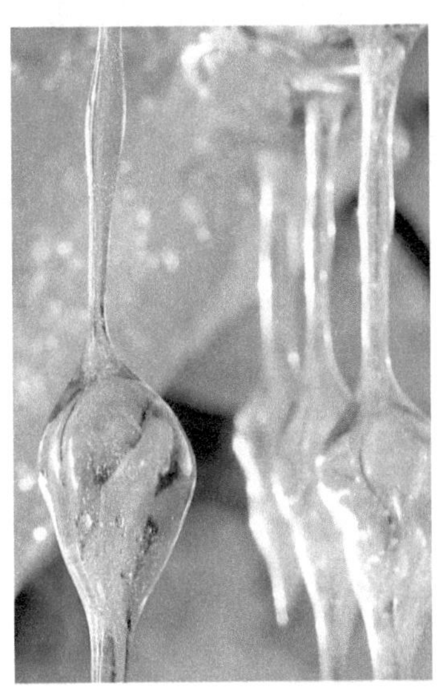

SCREW CHOCOLATE
14 QUEER valentines to get you through February 14
by YYC Queer Writers
curated by M. Jane Colette
photography by Jennifer Weihmann

GENRES were made to be BROKEN
121, 104-1240 Kensington Rd NW
Calgary, Alberta T2N3P7 Canada

ISBN: 978-1-7751809-0-6 (trade paperback)
ISBN: 978-1-7751809-1-3 (e-book)
mjanecolette.com/ScrewChocolate

for all our loves

CONTENTS

MOUNTAINS & MOMENTS

T

I

I am at a barbeque. Sticky in the evening, legs glowing sunshine against white short shorts and baking in the sputter of backyard campfire. I am the show piece tonight. I've been introduced to Geophysicist's friends, all of whom know exactly how crazy I am. One of them asks me if he's bought a ring yet. He yelps when his girlfriend smacks him.

My fingers find Geo's in-between the lawn chairs, meeting in the dark and pulling me closer to his ear.

'Do you wanna get out of here?' I murmur.

We are cocaine strung and a powder keg of enthusiasm. Doing handstands and high kicks, chattering about business goals and his family. About meeting them.

'You're getting ahead of yourself.' I twist and turn on my stool, awkward but smiling because I like him.

He is also getting nose deep in trouble and his eyes shade crazy for a minute in the kitchen. Finally, his patience with me makes sense.

II

The whole day is romantic. I am cooling in the alpine air, hair curling in the damp of my neck when I see another rainbow. I beam at Geo.

The other rainbows hang over kilometres of mottled evergreen forest, suspended in the clouds by our perch on the nose of a mountain. A crowning glory to that moment he had me screaming naked in his lap; together alone amidst the peaks and hundreds of metres above red rice grain canoes.

III

I am humming with hunger and four glasses of Manhattans. Geo is sharp dressed, spoiling me at dinner under centuries-old wooden wine cabinets. Vaulted ceilings and matching windows capture sunset in the mountains like a picture frame. I am tipsy and he is sulking. Stuck on a short text from a grumpy friend.

'Don't worry about it,' I say again, soothing variation number nineteen.

This is getting ridiculous. I just want to tell him to shut

up and start enjoying himself but instead he tells me to get used to this if I'm going to keep dating him. I sit silent, sip the Bourgogne, and await my veal.

IV

Sunlight splashes summer lakes and forested ranges. He is fishing and we are quiet. Calm and comfortable. We've been hanging casually between the back-road honey stand and the epic setup of his camping gear. I'm so unsure about how cool the weekend's been that his hand is a hot stain on my back when he peeks over my shoulder to admire pictures.

It is late and we are soaked in camp smoke when he calls to me across the site.

'I can't sit here looking at that ass anymore.'

Then he is in the tent, instructing me to take off my clothes, and I am melting to his mouth on my neck, fire running through my femurs and my shoulders. Banked heat all night, cuddled on our single cot.

The next day we don't touch much. I love hands-on affection; he is distant when he tells me he's 'jaded.' I know almost nothing else about his past.

V

The girl-squirrels are racing around my head and the room between us. Again, he is quiet, packing, and I am doing my own thing; debating him as an idea but enjoying the food and the evening. I stop his preparations by sitting down next to him on the edge of the bed.

'Can I distract you for a moment?'

And he kisses me, this time soft and wet and welcome. Not the dry lips and quick peck he doles out outside of bed. My thoughts are still too loud to feel him, to loosen up. I wonder what I'm doing and why, here. Am I going to crack him open? But his hands are persistent and find every button until I am drowning in ecstasy and nothing speaks but my body.

Another fast kiss when he sneaks out in the early morning. I wake alone in his apartment later, lock-up instructions and a towel at the ready. Easy, I guess.

*By day, **T** is a... We're not supposed to tell you. By night, she's... We're not supposed to tell you that either. She writes at dusk and twilight, except when she doesn't.*

KARMA, IN PRONOUNS

MARZENA CZARNECKA

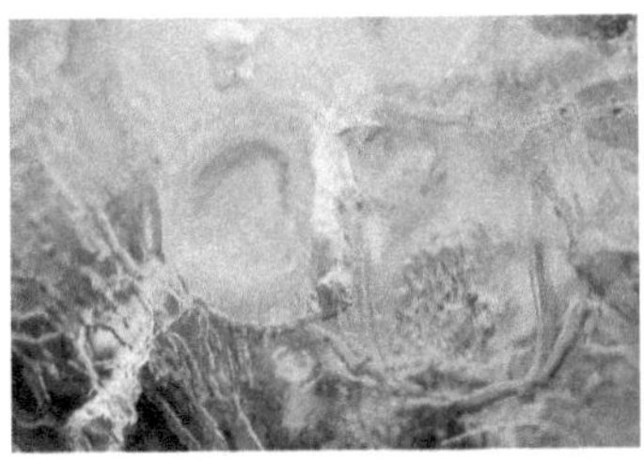

I

The insides of my thighs are punctured
with little round bruises, each the size
of a puckered mouth. 'Who are those
from,' they ask, touching them tenderly
then pressing hard, to hurt, in jealousy,
anger.

II

'They're from practicing the Crow,' is

the truth but as I speak it, they
already see another lover between
my thighs and jab a thumb into the
perfect circle of my elbow's imprint,
to punish.

III

I would bite the transgressing hand,
but why? Instead I move into the
thumb, meet their eyes, and watch
the demon consume them, transform him
into her, an insecure girl who cannot bear
to share.

IV

A few months later, I will become her,
feeling what she feels, tears welling
up in my eyes when I find a mark
on your body I did not make, ashamed
of the intensity of my possessiveness,
helpless.

❧

***Marzena Czarnecka** really hates yoga, and wishes English had either more or fewer pronouns. She talks in pictures on Instagram as @NothingByTheBook and sends the world postcards from Cuba and her kitchen via NothingByTheBook.com.*

THE LONG COMMUTE

L. SARA BYSTERVELD

The #72 bus. Each morning at 5:36 it picked me up from the corner directly below my apartment balcony. Most days I was the first passenger or very close to it, and on those days I always chose the same seat, halfway back, facing forward, next to the window with one seat between the aisle and me. I had taken this bus to work five mornings a week for two years and I knew the regulars. They would board the bus as we made our way toward downtown: the woman in the support hose who smelled like bread, the three young guys dressed for light industrial work, the middle-aged man on his way home from the night shift, always with a Newsweek or Time magazine. Others came and went.

She had been taking the seat next to me for a week when I started to think we may have a new regular. She was always listening to her music, and I normally read a book, but I noticed her and after two weeks I expected her to sit next to me each morning.

I did find it odd that she always sat next to me. Well, not always—sometimes, someone else would get there first, but normally the seat next to me was free and she took it. I didn't dwell on it much though.

After about a month of sitting beside her, something odd happened. She was listening to her music as always, and that morning, I was listening to mine too. We each had a bag on our lap, a hand on either side holding it in place.

Our hands touched.

Only, instead of pulling away, we just let them touch. My whole body went tense; I became acutely aware of my breathing and of everyone around us. Suddenly I noticed that she smelled nice, like moss and musk and spices. It was subtle but I realized then that I looked forward to this—to her scent—to *her*—each day.

We rode, fingers grazing, until we reached my stop.

After that, I couldn't get her out of my head. I thought about her all day; I couldn't ignore how turned on I was by the thought of her. I pictured her that night in bed, as I tried to fall asleep quickly so I would be back on the bus as soon as possible.

We never spoke. After that first touch, things progressed as far as they could on a bus, in plain view, quite quickly. We were soon holding hands each morning, neither of us speaking, her listening to music and me either reading or staring out the window.

What a strange thing, holding hands. It seems like the

most innocent of acts, but holding hands with her was one of the most sexual experiences of my life. Her thumb would trace my palm and I would feel myself grow wet. I began to carry an extra set of underwear to work with me. I tried to communicate to her, through my hand, that I wanted so badly to taste her, to fuck her, to hold her against me as she came. I thought she might be getting the message because she was communicating with me quite clearly as well; through her touch she showed me how softly her hands would explore my body, examining dips and curves, and the hard pressure she would employ as needed. And she continued to sit beside me and hold my hand.

Some days, she would tease me. A bare leg crossed in my direction, her hand brushing my breast as she settled into the seat, her foot on my calf as we rode. I didn't know her name, I didn't know where she worked. The more time went by, the less it felt like I could talk to her. But I thought about her constantly.

The ride home was always lonely. After a long day behind a desk, it was a disappointment to ride home alone with just my book or music to amuse me. I tried a few times to take the bus at a different time; I left work early on a few occasions and stayed late—then really late—a few others. I never caught her on the ride home. I needed a way to break up my day, something to look forward to after work.

So I joined a gym.

It was near my office, walking distance, and it had a sauna, which was one of my requirements, since a stint in the sauna could keep me warm for hours afterwards on long winter nights. I started going most nights after work, some nights taking a class and on others, jogging on the treadmill. I also went on weekends when I had the time.

It was a Sunday morning. Valentine's Day, actually, though I tried not to think about it. I had spent Saturday volunteering at a Valentine's Day food drive, and I was sore and tired from lifting crates of food. I decided to hit up the Sunday morning yoga class.

Afterward, muscles pliable and lengthened, back relaxed, I headed to the sauna. Everyone else from the class was in a rush to get to Valentine's brunch or something, and cleared out quickly, so the sauna was empty as I stepped in, naked. I spread a small towel on a bench to one side and sat down, closing my eyes.

I was thinking about the rest of my day and how I needed to pick up some groceries when I heard someone enter the sauna. I opened my eyes and saw her standing there in front of me, just as I'd pictured her every night for almost two months now, only so much better, now real, softer, a more generous curve here and a more beautiful definition there…

She still didn't speak. She just walked over, spread her own small towel on the bench beside me, and sat down, closing her eyes. As if we were riding on the bus again, her hand found mine, squeezing it tightly for a few seconds before she let her fingers trace the length of my arm, up and down, so lightly. It seemed to me that she intended to take it slowly, but two months of build-up was simply too much. We both leaned in. And that was that.

While we kissed, her hand traveled from my neck, downward between my breasts, and came to my belly, where her fingertips stroked back and forth. I tried to focus on kissing her, pretty easy as she bit my lip and kissed me the way I hoped she would soon be fucking me, but I did keep getting distracted by the thought that someone could walk in at any moment.

Still, I had been waiting for this long enough though that I really didn't care.

Her body was so beautiful. I stopped kissing her and cupped her breast, tracing her nipple with my thumb. She sighed. I kissed and bit her neck, pinching her nipple between my thumb and forefinger and felt myself grow even wetter when she sighed again. I moved slowly and deliberately, well aware how incredible this situation was.

I kissed down her chest to her breast, kissing beneath it and in her cleavage and finally taking her nipple into my mouth. It was so hard. I flicked it with my tongue and let my hand move down to her thigh. Her legs were closed, and I ran my hand from her knee to her groin, along her inner thigh, pressing my fingers gently into the crux of her thighs. She sighed again, and spread her legs just a little, enough for me to rub her clit. She spread her legs a little more in response, and I could finally feel how wet she was. I slid two fingers deep inside her and rubbed her g-spot as she let out a little yelp. She was so wet, and I knew I was too.

I needed to taste her. I climbed down off my bench and knelt on the bench below her, between her legs. I slowly licked her pussy from the bottom up, circling her clit with the tip of my tongue a few times once I was there. Again I slid two fingers, then three, inside her, fucking her as I sucked. She was squirming on the bench, fingers in my hair as I lapped at her. Each stroke of my fingers brought another, more appreciative moan, and I took her clit back into my mouth, sucking gently and licking up and down as she moaned louder. She tried hard to be quiet as she came but I felt her tighten around my fingers, her whole pussy pulsing around my hand. The taste of her combined with her throbbing cunt was probably the most beautiful moment I've ever experienced. I lingered for a minute or two, not wanting to withdraw or leave her taste or scent, her soft stomach. I knew that someone could catch us, so soon I hopped back onto the bench beside her.

She laid her head on my shoulder and whispered, 'I come here every Sunday morning.'

I knew that now, I would too.

❧

__L. Sara Bysterveld__ answers to Lindsay (her very good reason for the pretentious pen name can be found at lsarabysterveld.com), except when she doesn't answer at all because she is hiding from her five kids/step-kids, two partners, two cats, two rodents, two snails, and one tarantula. She was voted 'Most Likely to Publish a Book' and 'Most Likely to Be a Syndicated Columnist' at her journalism college graduation party, immediately before jumping into the pool fully clothed. She's still working on those goals and feels reasonably confident, at least after a couple of drinks, that she might achieve them one day.

Connect with Lindsay at Facebook.com/lsarabysterveld, find her on Twitter and Instagram as @linsybyster, and visit her blog, WeTheDancers.com

IT HAPPENS LIKE THIS

DANA STAN

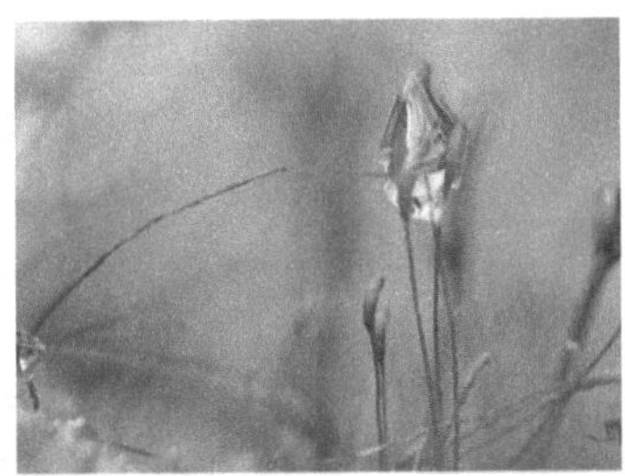

It all started with the spark of a lighter—a cigarette being lit and the smoke twirling lazily into the night. I breathed it in for the first time in almost a year. It rushed down my body and left me light-headed. The club's music thumped against the walls and the chatter outside was noisy but you were silent, staring out across the road at someplace far off in your mind. Was it then that something made my heart shift in your direction? I don't remember because I was drunk and not at all in touch with my feelings. I had come to a point in my life where I would have preferred to throw them away than to know them at all. Or was it when you took my hand—your voice so troubled, still, but your touch so caring?

What is it that first makes a river fork in another direction? Something small, perhaps. A shift in land. A surplus of water. Or, something internal, like a bank that just disintegrates and gives way over time. There were signs, absolutely, that something was giving way inside me. But at the same time, the new current seemed to just appear one day out of nowhere—like an earthquake breaking apart the ground for a new path. When I woke the next morning in my own bed, with my own girlfriend, everything had changed.

All of a sudden, your eyes took up so much space in my mind. I wasn't even sure what colour they were, at first, but I couldn't get them out of my head. My video game characters started to look like you—as if my hands just wanted to mold and re-create you in any way they could. But it was nothing more than a crush, I was sure, so I held it close to my breast as my own secret and, for the first few days, cuddled into my girlfriend at night with a clear conscience.

A week later, it wasn't getting any better and before I knew it, the guilt was so sharp and toxic that it hurt to breathe. I was abandoning her—my love, my lover—and drifting away down the current. She could feel it and tried to pull me back but it was no use. Maybe we were just going through a bad time in the relationship; maybe we just needed some space? I thought of everything as I drove down highways with the music blasting, bawling my eyes out. My best friend and I sat on a point overlooking the city, smoking again for the first time since that night, and I was sure that these feelings were just a manifestation of my dissatisfaction.

It had nothing to do with you.

How could it?

I didn't even know you.

(But I knew, I now knew the colour of your eyes. Intimately.)

I thought I had created a fantasy girl inside my own head, one who would give me everything my real girlfriend couldn't. One who looked into my eyes and touched my soul at the same time. But it was ridiculous to fall in love with a stranger thinking that they were some warrior princess come to sweep you off your feet. I knew it. I knew it. But something kept pulling me back over and over again, and every time I saw you, it got worse.

You were perfect—on paper and in person. I loved your insecurities and your flaws; I loved the way you asked these blunt questions but still got shy when you were talking about yourself. I loved the way you smiled. Soon, you completely took over my heart and I didn't know what to call this anymore. A crush, still? Infatuation?

Love?

I tore apart my relationship trying to get to the root of these feelings. I dug up the root, dissected it into pieces, and then I dug around in my insides until I was nothing but stripped bones... and I still can't get you out of my head. My girlfriend is casually seeing someone else now and everyone is telling me to get back in the game—to find someone else who will distract me and take my mind off of you.

Maybe one day the images of you burned in my mind will fade.

But today is Valentine's Day and I sit here, smoking, thinking only about your brown eyes.

❧

Dana Stan *is working on her second novel and that's why she's started smoking again. It has nothing to do with anyone's brown eyes. Or does it?*

TRY

M. JANE COLETTE

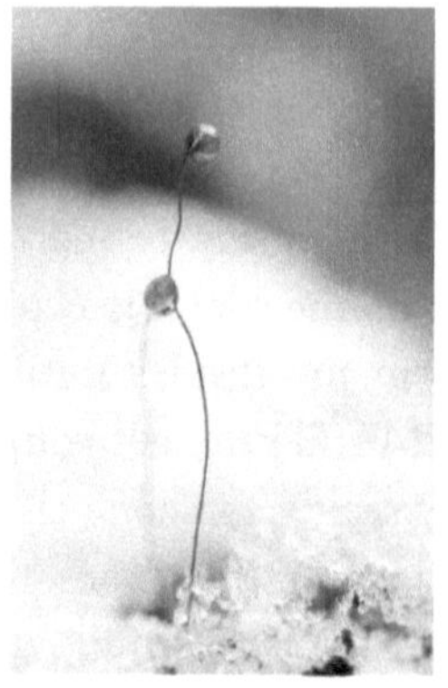

Once, I begged a love to stay.
It was awful.

I had abandoned all pride, all dignity, all reason. I wasn't a woman—I wasn't a human. I was a mass of love, lust, and unspent desire.

And I begged.

I begged, abased.

It did not, of course, stay.

Once love decides to leave, once one lover is done, the

end is unavoidable. The one who still loves can do nothing. Nothing.

Yet I think, perhaps—no, I know, I *know*: we must try.

I begged. Abased. Utterly subjugated. Completely broken.

I failed, adding the burn of humiliation to the cold of rejection.

And yet, that moment—me, on my knees, stripped naked, exposed, no armour remaining, no secrets left, no part of me kept back, nothing in reserve, everything spent, everything thrust into the hands, thrown at the feet of a withdrawing love—I would not trade that moment for anything.

Let me be clear—I would rather die than repeat it, willingly.

And yet—that moment—me, begging, abased, exposed, nothing held back—I have never felt more alive.

Afterwards, burned, rejected, I wanted to die. For a while, anyway. Out of shame. Out of pain.

And yet, and yet—underneath the shame, the pain—I was so fully alive.

I don't know if I will ever dare that again.

I don't know if I will ever dare to beg a love to stay.

I'm older now—more seasoned, more experienced, and so either wiser or more cynical. I know that when a love decides to leave, nothing can make it stay. And I'm not sure I would be capable of engaging in the dramatic futility of that final assault, throwing my all at love's departing feet.

To what purpose?

To show to myself that I loved enough to fight, to beg.

That I loved enough... to suffer.

You will leave anyway, when love has left, no matter what I do.

Today, right now, you are here. I am here.

So is love. And when it leaves—should it leave, as it might, for love often does—I hope you love enough to beg.

I hope I love enough to beg.

Once love decides to leave, once one lover stops loving, the one who still loves can do nothing.

Nothing.

But we must try.

Happy Valentine's Day, love.

***M. Jane Colette** writes tragedy for people who like to laugh, comedy for the melancholy, and erotica for men and women who like their fantasies real. She generally writes much more filthy things, but isn't it good to know she can also be romantic and sappy? Connect with @mjanecolette on Twitter and Instagram or send an old school email to TellMe@mjanecolette.com.*

SUNRISE

BROOKE NICHOLAS

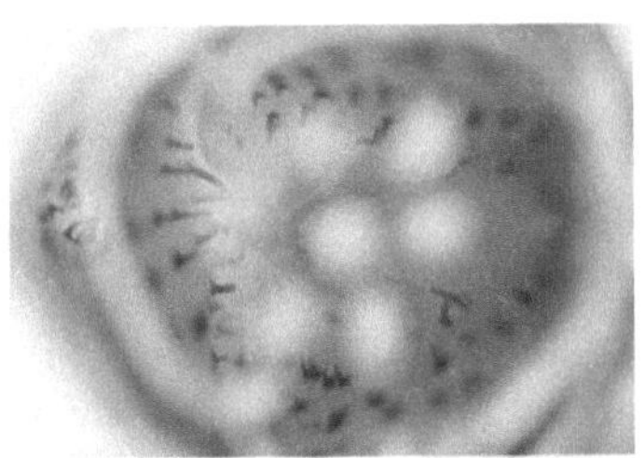

I

The night was so dark.

It was in its darkness that a love was broken. The bonds were not strong enough to last the test of time. The light from the heart not strong enough to guide them home.

Perhaps they had wandered too far from each other, got separated, and then could not find their way back.

They got lost in the dark.

But it was also in the darkness that they found what they were looking for.

II

As the sun comes up on a new day, its rays find them. Not together, but happy.

In the darkness, they find the light.

III

I wish I could have been your light to always guide you home.

But I am happy that we have each found what we need. Our journey was not in vain. For if we had not walked the path together, in the dark, we would not have been able to see the light at its end.

❧

Brooke Nicholas *was born in Dawson Creek, BC, lives in Calgary, Alberta, and still thinks of Nelson, BC as home. She's been dating since she was 15 and hunting since she's been 31. She usually writes stories about wolves. This is not one of them.*

WANT

T

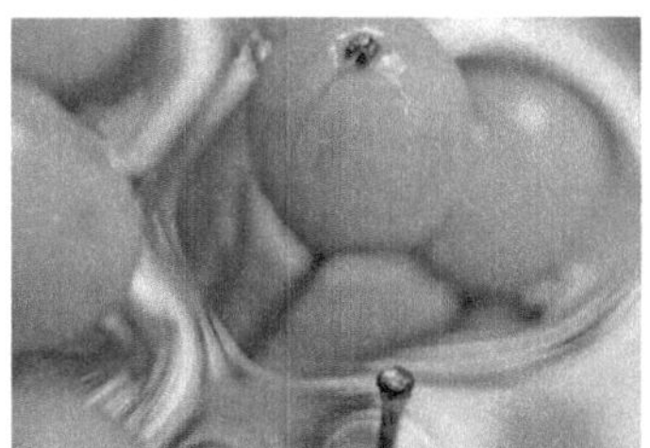

His lips are sweet with me and the sheets and his fingers are covered in my cum and trailing my skin gently. Nightstand light glows soft over my words.

'I don't know what I want right now.'

The tail end of the jumpy, rambling explanation that is my love life. I might want a boyfriend, but I really don't want to feel tied to that reality. I might want a hot one-nighter, but I really am tired of blah bar boys. I might want a date, but I really would rather spend the time on me. High School Cutie is single like spring grass and not good at women. He is easy going and eager to please; drunk victory fist pumping when I took him home last time from our boys' night out. He is my short-term solution.

I kick him out once we've used both condoms and send his short, soft frame through my door with a pat on the ass and a twinkle of my fingers. He also happens to be good at getting me off.

Four days later, my Old Friend is picking me up. We chatter all night long around champagne glasses in a box-filled apartment kitchen. I am reconnecting with Old Friend with seventeen-year-old Pirate-sized rum shots and these boys are my favourite kind of hooligans. When I lay down on the mattress in the spare room at 7 am, I am smiling with the satisfaction of deep night political debate and ski dreaming.

I find Old Friend in my bed a few minutes later. His heart beats like thunder under my palm and I curl into the crooks on his body like a happy cat. I am half asleep and glowing with love.

'I can't sleep,' he whispers. 'And I'm horny. Want to fool around?'

'If you promise not to be weird about it later.'

A year later and I still adore the way he kisses; I melt so fast into his greasy beard and lanky hair. His hands burn over my hips and into my panties. But he doesn't have a condom and when I hesitate his dick loses interest. I tumble off him, flopping long and throwing an arm over his chest. I kiss the spot where his cheek crumbles into laugh lines.

'You really know how to treat a lady.'

He gets too hot for my sheets, but comes back two hours later. My nose is pressed into his neck again when I ask him if he's still interested. No, no. He basically hasn't been hard since I turned him down. Tough break.

Back between my own blankets deleting Tinder messages, I realize that I am glad it didn't work. Realize that we are sex like cold pizza, and he doesn't have an appetite. He is my Old

Friend—mountain man and shotgun sharer and I like it that way. I realize that maybe it's not that I don't know what I want right now, but maybe that I know exactly what I want instead.

❧

T doesn't always know who she is, but she usually knows what she wants. Right now, she wants to know what she wants, but she also knows that when you want to know what you want too intensely, you don't get it, on principle.

GET THE FUCK UP AND LOVE

DALLAS BARNES

So here's the thing…

When you are crazy (and I am, and it's mine, and I fucking claim the word), you question everything about yourself.

Some questions that have actually occurred:

- I know my throat is raw and I can't breathe but seriously depression does that, right?
- Did I really make plans to go out tonight or did I just make that up in my head?
- Who am I?
- Where am I?
- I can't believe I said that... is she going to hate me forever?
- Am I the only person in this world and everyone else a part of my imagination?
- Why am I the ugliest person in the world?

So when you are in the here and now, wanting and working your fucking ass off to be better (day by day), you really have to figure your damn head out in order to function like a human.

The problem lies in your ability to be ok with yourself. When you question everything around you, you forget how to understand yourself as a thinking thing, a human, a valid voice. You forget (in fact may have never known) that how you think and feel is ok.

When you are sick... you are sick. Fucking period. You didn't make up the 103 degree fever or the constant stream of… well, you get the point. You did not make this up because you are not some superhuman with the ability to inflict imaginary germs on yourself.

When you are upset... you are upset. Your set of okayness values was not met... you're sad, angry, frustrated. To feel that is ok... more than ok. When you close off your heart for long periods of time to avoid potential cataclysmic events that most people call life (you just can't deal) and have the fucking courage to open your heart up and have it be stomped on... by all means... MOTHERFUCKING CRY!

Cry for your delicate yet powerful heart, for its ache but

also for its courage to open itself up to possibility... to beautiful life! You have become a part of the majority (but are so happy that you're still a little weird).

When you question your set of values... just stop. Your values are your own. When a girlfriend (now ex) tells you that you are 'too gay' (she was the one with the mullet) or another one tells you that 'you are just too much to handle'... fuck 'em. Fuck them and their bullshit attack on who you are. Fuck them for not embracing the everything that is you. You earned this badge... you fucking earned it.

When you think you are not good enough and feel like you have to hide so you won't be hurt... go out! Test yourself, force yourself. Not everyone is going to like you and even if you go on some manic tangent (because you are after all deliciously crazy) don't fucking worry about it. Not everyone is going to like you, but those who do are yours for life.

When your girlfriends (now exes) cheat on you once, twice, three fucking times... get out. Don't hate yourself because you went back... you went back because you believe (and still do) in the sanctity of commitment and love. You were willing to fight for it even when it wasn't pretty. You loved and loved hard and were willing to try... so don't lose faith in your potential to love and be loved back. Your person(s) are out there.

When you look in the mirror and seriously fucking hate what you are looking at (and may go for days without ever looking), don't beat yourself up. Just live... maybe without looking for a while until you're ready (baby steps). You hate what you see because you are not looking at yourself. That person is not you. That is the sad, beaten down, and exhausted you.

You, the real you, the full you, are hiding in there... you will come out... (still working on that).

Remember that this reflection is what is holding you back

from doing things... being alive... drinking with drag queens, protesting bullshit homophobes, dancing until you forget that there is gravity, loving and being loved by your people, finding the people you yearn for.

The problem lies with the fact that you have not been able to be ok because some ridiculous piece of shit chemical in your brain is tearing you apart. You have been fighting for so long just to walk out the door and survive... you've gotta fight. You have to fight for yourself... for your rightful place in the world. No one is going to do this for you... but if you let them, the good ones will help you along the way.

But you have to let them in.

You have to trust the process.

You have to live.

You have to fight.

And if you feel like your whole world is going to crumble... because it will... we aren't immune... fucking cry. Cry alone, cry with friends, just cry with every ounce of you. And then take a breath... and get up, and let love reign.

❧

***Dallas Barnes** is a queer, cisgender, feminist, activist, and writer. She writes about life—its downfalls, turmoils, hilarities, and elations. Her experience with mental illness and all things queer makes her writing real, raw, and in your face. Dallas lives in Calgary, Alberta, with her cat Grizzly and tweets as @salladsenrab.*

ELIZABETH

NOLA SARINA

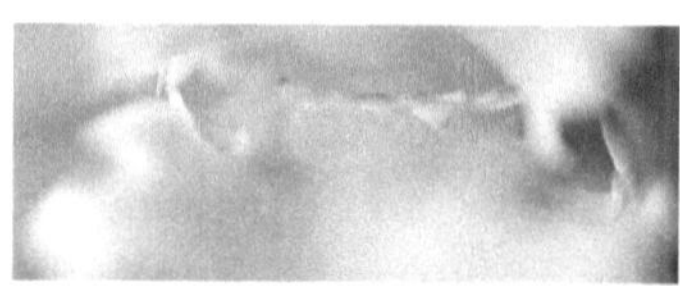

I meet Elizabeth the first day I finally commit to an $85 monthly membership at a twenty-four-hour all-women's gym. All I'm thinking about is the ellipticals and the sauna. Also, shedding at least twenty-five pounds. I'm not interested, not at all, in the possibility of meeting someone.

Then Elizabeth hops on the bike next to me, and even though I swear to myself I'm not going to check her out, I can't resist a glance, then two. I try to keep it to under a dozen.

She is on the bike next to me—she could have chosen any bike in the row. I am smack in the middle of twelve bikes, but no, she chooses the one next to me. It means nothing. I read nothing into it. She steals glances at me, too.

Something funny happens when you forget your MP3 player in the cup holder of your SUV and don't take the time to retrieve it before you start a workout: you hear everything around you. And from the moment Elizabeth picks up her speed on the bike, I hear every nuance, every note of her breath. Passing through her lips, into her body, quickening with exertion.

Her breath intensifies as our workout progresses, and so does mine. I push my speed to distract myself from my desire to glance sideways, again and again. Images dance through my head: her gasping on my bedsheets, her fingers clutching the pillowcase.

I push myself harder. And harder. And so does she. Pretty soon, we are panting so hard we are almost moaning with exertion, voice slipping into every inhale.

I don't stop... pedalling... until she does.

'Hi,' she says to me as my feet find their roots on the floor again. 'I'm Elizabeth.'

I swallow hard, averting my eyes from hers. 'Um. Charity,' I stammer.

Her fingertips touch my chin, and when I finally meet her eyes—her face framed by one half-curled black strand that escapes her ponytail, and eyes shimmering in a way I can't ignore—I never want to stop looking at her.

She is breathtaking, and not only because we've just crushed two miles on the bikes. Her skin is darker than mine, smooth and shining with sweat, and as she holds my chin and cracks a smile that holds a devious glimmer of intensity, my cardio picks up even more.

Yes. I'm still panting.

'We should have coffee, Charity. Don't you think?'

I nod.

I don't remember how we decide, exactly, that we should have coffee at my place. But we do, and there we are, in the lobby, me and Elizabeth, this woman I've just met and am now taking up to my apartment.

Her eyes never deviate from me as the elevator takes its gradual glide up the cables. My keys jingle in my hand as I fidget with them, and I push the button again just to give my fingers something to do. I swear I feel Elizabeth smiling at my impatience. I've never felt someone's smile burning into the back of my head before. But it's not only my head she's looking at. It's my neck, my back… like fingertips trailing down my skin, penetrating my jacket, awakening me inside.

The elevator reaches my floor, and my heels lift as it stops. I glance back at Elizabeth. She still wears that sinful grin, her eyes only on me.

I unlock the door to my apartment and let Elizabeth in first. I drop my purse, lock the door behind us, and she slides off her shoes.

'Um, coffee?' I ask. I fidget with my fingers in front of my body.

'Love some,' Elizabeth says. Her grin tugs up more on one side than the other, giving her a single dimple. 'But I could really use a shower first.'

My face heats a billion degrees. 'Oh, yeah, sure.' I step aside and point. 'It's right through there.'

A bright, quick laugh escapes Elizabeth's lips. 'Okay.' She takes my hand and gives it a tug, her eyebrows lifting in question.

I follow. My heart pounds, nerves lighting up with electricity along every inch of my body.

We're naked in a flurry of sports bras and yoga pants. Those eyes... deep, deep brown, and I swear in the fluorescent light of the bathroom, I see gold flecks in her irises… they never stop dancing over my shoulders, my waist. Then, my breasts. My arms, my hands.

Elizabeth sets the water to a comfortable warm, not too hot. I step into the stream with her, and my breath grows sharper. Hers sets an even pace. She walks her fingertips along the back of my shoulder, urging me to turn and face her. She rakes her gaze over me, totally exposed now, her hands twisting with mine as she pulls us closer together. The water runs over both of us, and as our bodies connect in the middle, heat flashes in my core. I bite the corner of my lip, nerves thudding through my veins. How can she be so calm, so steady? I want to make her breathe like she did in the gym, make her pant and gasp until her voice emerges in her breath, that sound that hooked me to her and will not let me go.

Yes, that's what I want. My nerves fire into urgency, and I turn her, press her back to the tile, pin her hands beside her head, and kiss her.

She kisses back, her lips gentle and soft, while mine beg for more. I release her hands and let them fall to her shoulders, my thumbs resting on the side of her neck, while hers find my hips, glide around to my back, and tug me tight to her body. The slick of the water between us drives my need, but still her breathing is even, smooth. My lips work down to her neck, and she drops her head gently back against the tile. A quiet sound escapes her mouth.

There. I can get to her the way she gets to me. Now I know I can. My hands hold her sides, my grip possessive, and I let my fingertips trail slowly down the centre of her chest. She watches me, her eyes on fire with arousal, and my fingertips dip lower until I touch that soft patch of hair. Lower, still.

Her breath leaves her in a single rush, and my fingers graze her in all the places throbbing between my own legs right now. Elizabeth sucks in a gasp, and when she lets out a sharp moan, triumph soars through me, and I stroke her gently at first, then firmer, then faster. Her hands twist into my hair as her legs struggle to hold her up. I duck my head to her neck, my lips moving of their own accord, tasting, teasing. She's all smooth, delicious silk everywhere I touch. I slip my arm around her waist and hold her up while my fingers drive her on and on, and when she cries out and clenches around me, waves rippling through my own centre with pleasure, her balance failing, I catch her, holding her tight while she comes back down to Earth.

Her mouth parts against my shoulder. Her gasping morphs into kisses. The way she clings to me shifts to caresses. Her lips part beside my ear, and she whispers, 'Your turn.'

By the time we're done, we're both wrinkly from the water, red-faced, and grinning. We towel off, and as Elizabeth squeezes water out of her hair, I meet her eyes, unintimidated. They glow with satisfaction.

'Do you go to the gym every Tuesday?' I ask her.

Elizabeth grins. 'And Thursday.'

'We should have coffee again on Thursday,' I say.

We do.

***Nola Sarina** is a paranormal romance, dark fantasy, and erotica author from Alberta, Canada. She loves weaving romances that leave you breathless and challenge typical relationships with the most mind-blowing twists. Nola is the author of the spicy hot dark fantasy Vesper series. She is also the co-author of* Wild Hyacinthe *and* THE CORE *with friend Emily Faith.* THE CORE *invites every reader to throw stereotypes out the window, strip down, and get dirty.*

Follow Nola on Twitter @nolasarina.

INSTRUCTIONS

PW ZELLIE

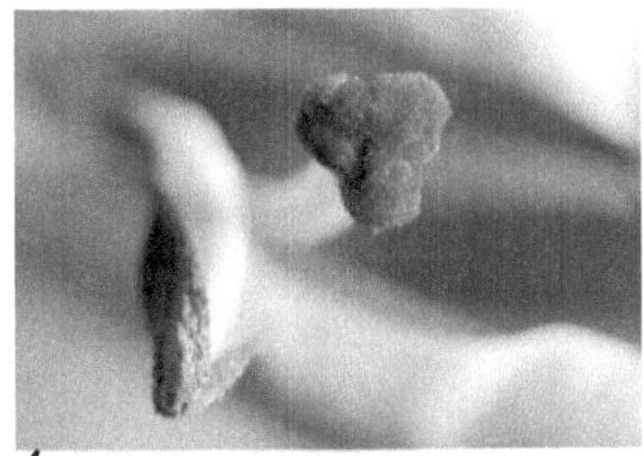

Kissing, full body contact, legs interlaced, moving slowly, pleasure increases.

Sitting up, moving so that clit to clit is enjoyed.

Weight back on arms, so that more pressure can be applied.

So warm, so wet, so welcome.

Laying back now, both on our backs, remembering her pleasure as I forget mine, then forgetting hers as I lose myself in mine. Arms grasped around legs for more leverage, juices flowing freely, soaking the bed.

Hearing her moan makes me want to see her.

Pulling myself up, still gyrating, her legs in a double V, I am almost kneeling, one knee near her ribs, one under her leg, hands on her breasts as I lower myself, slowly, to kiss her mouth.

Laying right on her as I kiss her jaw, nibble her ear, then bite her neck.

Upright again, now one heel against her rosebud, sole of the other foot down by her head, the most intense yet, clit to clit, labia to labia, entranceway to entranceway, our juices mixing completely, never been so wet, either of us.

No sense of decorum as both of us thrust wildly, moaning madly, then drowning in eyes as she comes, wild-eyed, screaming huskily.

She bites my foot.

I turn slightly to rest my head on her knee, my back towards her just for a moment, it is too long to be away, so I turn and lower myself to kiss her mouth as she pants for breath.

Then leg moves to leg, and we are side by side again, still kissing, still touching. I move her hair from her face and kiss her all over.

We should be spent but we start again, kissing deeply...

Cleverly disguised as a middle-aged nondescript librarian type, ***PW Zellie*** *glides through life, unremarked upon but grinning slyly, enjoying all life's yummy secrets.*

UNMENTIONABLES

ALYSSA LINN PALMER

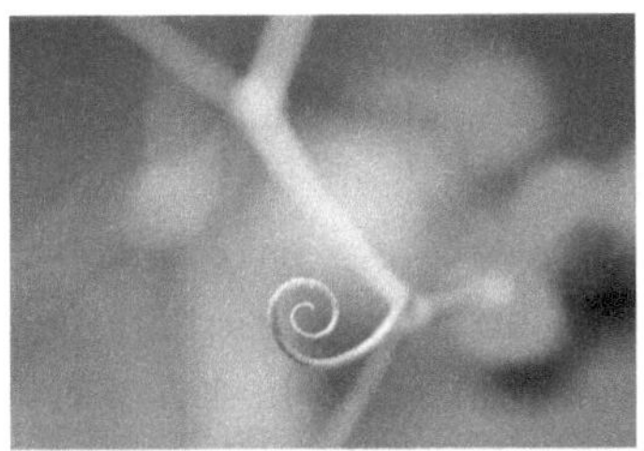

Valentine's Day eve. Vee moved in just a few weeks ago, a huge step for both of us, and one I still worry about. Not about us, never. We're solid. But about others, and their opinions, yes, sometimes. What is a woman of my age (late forties, if you must know) doing with a girl of twenty-one? My conservative-looking self with the punk rock Vee. She's lean and leggy, scattered tattoos and a Monroe stud. Right now, her usually-blue hair has streaks of pink, 'for the occasion,' she said.

I have an article due tomorrow—what sadist gives Valentine's Day as a deadline? —but I can't figure out how to finish it. I have been spending the last hour pacing between the kitchen and the office, occasionally stopping to peer out the window and down the fire escape to the grimy alley below. Once I opened the window to hear the bustle of NYC, the honking traffic, the people. But nothing has worked.

On my next pace, back past the bedroom, a flash of movement catches the corner of my eye, a bit of blue. I pause, retreat, linger just outside the door. Vee is changing for bed.

She draws her shirt up over her head—one of her usual rock band tees—and I want to put my tongue to each of the stars tattooed up the side of her ribcage, feel each bump, each indentation. To kiss the red marks from her bra, which she barely needs. She bends at the waist to tug off her skinny jeans. I smile to myself and bite my lip to keep from chuckling as she curses and hops on one foot. They're so snug round the calves that it's always a challenge. I've experienced that challenge myself, pulling vainly when she's sprawled on the bed, wanting nothing more than to get her naked.

Vee flings the jeans into the laundry hamper, and her socks follow, one after the other, hitting the wall before falling in. This is why people talk; she's over the legal age, but she still finds delight in simple, sometimes childish things.

I don't care.

I do, but I'm learning not to, trying to follow her example.

Vee does a sudden shimmy, her fingers in the waist elastic of her boyshorts, and I snap back to attention. She looks over her shoulder.

I'm caught.

'Alex...' she calls, a smile widening, her stud glinting in the lamplight. Her eyebrow quirks up, an unmistakable come-hither. Subtlety isn't Vee's thing. Though we've done this so many times before, my mouth goes dry, and my knees go weak. I'm instantly wet, instantly wanting.

So cliché. My mother would shake her head. 'Oh, Alex,' she'd say.

To hell with them all.

We've done it, Vee's here with me, I'm here with her, and it's the best decision I've ever made in my life.

'Stop thinking so much,' Vee chides, coming forward to grasp my hand.

I start to speak, but she pulls me forward and wraps her arms around my neck, bringing her lips to mine, pressing her tongue past my lips. It's wet and hot and fantastic and I can't remember what I was worried about.

I flick her bra clasp and then cup her breasts, her nipples tightening under my palms. She shivers delightfully, letting out a low moan when I lightly pinch those hardened nipples. We shift and she lets the bra fall away.

Pale skin, so pale it almost has a blue tinge to it, one that isn't a side effect of her hair colour. And those light pink nipples. I put my hands at the small of her back, silently demanding that she arch towards me, and I bend to flick one nipple with my tongue. Vee's clutching the cloth of my shirt at the shoulders, and I drop one hand down into her boy shorts, clasping those slender buttocks.

It's so easy to tease her sex, brushing my fingertips against its wetness. She squirms, but only to get closer.

'Alex...' she says again, but this time it's breathy, needy.

We back up, towards the bed, and she falls back onto the coverlet, arms and legs like a starfish.

'Clothes, Alex,' she reminds me. I take a moment to unbutton my shirt and let it fall, and then my jeans—my much more sensible boot-cut jeans—drop too. Her gaze devours me, and she holds out her hand again. I kneel on the bed between her legs, and when she tries to remove my front-clasp bra, I pin her hand to the bed.

'Not yet.'

Vee subsides, but only for now.

I want her underwear off. She helps, lifting her hips. I toss the scrap of fabric aside, bending again, kissing the jut of her hip bone, the hollow, the soft curve of her stomach just above what little is left of her pubic hair. She'd shaved it into a heart yesterday, just for a laugh, and she's bare below the wisps. The dampness glimmers there, promising.

I hold her knees apart—not that she'd close them—and flick my tongue against that dampness, slowly, carefully, pleased at the quivering I cause. My sex is wanting, but I'll wait for my own satisfaction. I want to hear her gasps, her moans, her pleading. I flick again, and linger this time, and her hips cant towards me.

This is us, so perfectly us. I can never get enough.

'More,' she demands. I comply.

She tastes like no other as I delve into her soft folds, flicking her clitoris, then lightly penetrating her before I withdraw, hearing her gasp.

I only give her a moment to rest before I return, and this time I mean to have her come. I hold her thighs open, my thumbs in the hollows on either side of her sex. Her heat, her scent, her desperate little movements… I'm close to coming myself.

Vee squirms more, and her breathing is heavy now, almost panting. She's coming close to that cliff, to that moment of the rush, of the fall, of immediate pleasure. I want to prolong it, but she's gasping little pleas, and I do as she asks. I slip my index finger into her, pressing up, against her g-spot, stroking hard. She clenches around me, her gasps becoming an 'Oh God,' and then, 'Alex.' She shudders and spasms, but I don't stop, drawing out her orgasm as long as I can. She cries out again and I feel a new batch of spasms around my finger, another set of shivers. Her legs clamp around me as her hips arch up, seeking the most sensation possible.

Her chest heaves with her breathing, and her legs relax,

and she slides bonelessly to the bed, reminding me very much of a cat in the midst of a deep sleep. But her eyes open and she smiles, the most beatific smile.

'Weren't you going to save that for tomorrow?' she asks, her voice a whisper.

'It's close enough.' I glance at the clock. 12:02. It is.

'I had a surprise for you,' she says, and I sprawl out beside her, still in my bra and underwear. 'But it means getting rid of these.' She fingers the strap of my bra. I sit up and undo the clasp, sliding the straps down my arms and off. 'And these.' She snaps the elastic of my underwear. I stand up and take them off, tossing both items into the hamper.

'Always so neat,' she teases. She sits up, pushing her hands through her hair, the blue and pink a charming mess. She rises from the bed and goes to the armoire, to her side of it, opening a drawer and pushing aside her underwear.

'Sit down,' she says, and I do, perching on the edge of the bed.

Vee turns, and in her hand is a neat little box, tied in a glossy white ribbon. She places it in my hands.

'Open it.'

I don't know what to think. It isn't small enough to be jewelry. Or at least, I don't think so.

I carefully tug at the ribbon and remove it, setting it on the bed beside me. She watches as I open the box, and I know she's dying of anticipation. She loves giving gifts, seeing my surprise. As a result, I take my time.

There's tissue paper, also white, and it crinkles as I lift the folds.

Lace.

White lace.

My breath catches in my throat.

Vee perches beside me on the bed, leaning in against my arm. She catches a fold of the lace with a finger and lifts it, bringing to our gaze delicate thong panties. Below it in the box is a bra, with lace cups and underwire.

'Vee...' I start. I can see the tag, and I know it's expensive, more than she can likely afford.

'I want you in it,' she says. 'I've dreamed of it.'

She rises and pulls me to my feet with her, handing me the thong. I step into it and pull it up, smoothing the lace at my hips. She lifts the bra and slides it over my arms, stepping behind me to do up the clasp.

Then she nudges me towards our ensuite bathroom. I see myself, her hands at my waist, a vision in white lace.

'I want this under your wedding dress,' she whispers in my ear. 'Tomorrow, perhaps?'

I am speechless.

But I know the right answer. I've always known, ever since I met her.

It's us.

'Yes.'

❧

Alyssa Linn Palmer is a Canadian writer and freelance editor. She splits her time between a full-time day job and her part-time loves, writing and editing. She is a member of the Romance Writers of America, the Calgary RWA, and RRW (Rainbow Romance Writers). She has a passion for Paris and all things French, which is reflected in her writing. When she's not writing lesbian romance, she's creating the dark, morally flawed characters of the Le Chat Rouge series and indulging in her addictions to classic pulp fiction.*

Get to know her at AlyssaLinnPalmer.com or follow her on Twitter at @alyslinn.

THE SHY GIRL'S GUIDE TO SEXTING

M. JANE COLETTE

—Hi. :)

—I was just thinking about you too.

—Oh, you know. Stuff.

—Maybe... what were you thinking?

—Oh.

—Well... yes, maybe, a little shocked. I didn't expect you to be so... explicit?

—No, not offended, just...

—Oh.

—Mmmmm.

—No...

—no, really, I can't type that. I can't even THINK that!
—Oh...
—Yes.
—I am, I did.
—I really am doing it. Yes.
—Jesus.
—You...
—...are
—...unbelievable...
—Yes.
—Yes, soaked.
—OMFG, your mind...
—I can't.
—your tongue
—yes, just like that
—right there
—oh fuck
—more
—I want more.
—I can't...
—I just can't, I know you think I'm a prude, but I can't...
—oh... yes...
—please
—mmmmm
—yes, I love it...
—fingers
—two
—four
—no!
—yes...
—I don't know...
—ok...
—I am...
—I will...

—god...
—one more time...
—yes, like that...
—omfg
—a puddle
—yes...
—thank you?
—THANK YOU
—ok...
—yes :)
—I'm too fucking shy.
—really
—maybe next time?
—mmmmmmm
—oh yes
—K
—me too
—ttyl xo

❧

***M. Jane Colette** writes tragedy for people who like to laugh, comedy for the melancholy, and erotica for men and women who like their fantasies real. She's the author of the 'is it literature or is it porn' erotic romances* Tell Me, Consequences (of defensive adultery), *and* Cherry Pie Cure, *and the non-fiction collection of essays on language, taboos, and the business of writing,* CUNT versus PUSSY *(reissued in 2017 with the more library-friendly title* Rough Draft Confessions*). Connect with @mjanecolette on Twitter and Instagram or whisper secrets to her at TellMe@mjanecolette.com.*

DELIVERY

ELISA KAE

This was one of those days that Emily was glad she could work from home. It was a blustery mid-February afternoon and she was honestly relieved she wouldn't be inundated by throngs of co-workers asking about her plans for this pink and red holiday. She genuinely liked the people she worked with, but their questioning about her love life always got a little out of hand at this time of year.

Really, it was none of their business.

She was pouring herself another cup of coffee when she was interrupted by a knock at her door. Flutters filled her belly as she approached the entryway, and a smile stretched across her face when she opened the door to see a handsome young man standing there.

'Good afternoon, Emily.'

'Hello there, Tyler... so nice of you to come see me today.'

'Well, I couldn't avoid an opportunity to see your smiling face, could I?'

She laughed. 'No, I suppose you couldn't.'

'You always seem so happy to see me.'

'You do deliver, I'll say that much.'

'That is my job!' He beamed and handed her a package. 'Your online shopping habit does keep me busy. I'll probably see you next week. You have yourself a happy Valentine's Day!'

'You too,' she said as she closed the door and hurried with her parcel down the hall to her bedroom.

She split open the nondescript cardboard box and dug through the packing material until she freed a long silver case. Carefully laying it down on the bed, she lifted the magnetic lid and couldn't contain a coo of excitement. It was exactly as she had hoped: smooth matte purple silicone, long full shaft, with a lascivious bulbous head. Lifting it free, she tested the cool, firm resistance of the thick, fused rabbit ears jutting from the side. Feeling the resolute weight in her hand, her thumb intuitively caressed the buttons. She tested the controls, feeling her new lover hum to life. Her lips curled, and she hushed it back to stillness before settling into bed.

She laid back and shifted her body as she slipped out of her panties. The hem of her skirt fell up her thighs and settled around her waist. Her fingers dipped into the pot of coconut oil on her nightstand before they wandered down between her legs. They slid through her lips and mingled the slick new wetness with her own, enjoying the spreading heat. She built up her longing with gentle caresses and light touches, right where she liked them. She ran the full length of her finger up and down over her clit, dipping into her pussy before drawing it back up again, teasing just enough to make herself even hungrier for the suitor waiting so patiently beside her.

Her desire built and spread. She reached over, taking her new paramour in her hand. Stroking her wet fingers over its length, she felt it slick and warm before parting her labia. Oh, but it felt so good, and slipped so naturally into her wetness. She held her breath as each inch penetrated her in a smooth motion until the ears touched just below her clit, then slid up, nestling snugly against her. With the shaft pressed deep, she took a moment to feel the still fullness, to roll her hips and adapt to the invariable pressure before her thumb found the ignition.

It started as a low deep hum in the shaft, but she quickly cycled up to a more insistent vibration. The head rolled deep within her, massaging her core. She pushed her thighs apart and pressed it deeper before her thumb shifted to the other button and awoke the rabbit. Her back arched at the sudden power shocking over her, and she pulled it back, lifting the ears from her clit, causing the undulating head to slide to shallower places. She tipped her hips, stroking it over her sweet spot, but there was only so long she could last this way. The desire to feel that delicious swollen fullness compelled her to drive it deep again, the purring ears tapping her clit with each thrust.

The intensity of the stimulation was almost overwhelming but she wanted more. She ground it into herself, feeling the full vibrations up and over her clit with the deep thrumming inside, touching every part of her. She felt herself climb, tightening around the silky shaft as it opened her over and over again. She pulled herself closer, thrusting harder, and letting her gasping moans fill the room. She felt the bloom and kept going, hard, her pussy constricting around the undulations, the rabbit pressed tight to her, sliding up and back, flicking her clit with each pass, the vibrations sinking through her until her orgasm was inevitable. She pounded frantically until the only thing she could do was press it deep and let it take her over the edge. The quaking shakes exploded from her, ripping down her legs, up her body and out her open mouth. Her body arched and shuddered and as she pulled the beautiful creature from her body, her wetness ran down over her ass, soaking the sheets below her.

The smell of her sex hung heavy in the room and a lazy smile spread across her face as she came back to earth.

'Happy Valentine's Day, Bunny. I think I love you.'

❧

***Elisa Kae** is not filmed in front of a live studio audience. She contains adult content that may not be suitable for some audiences. Listener discretion is strongly advised.*

Speaking of listening, you can listen to Elisa on Soundcloud and follow her on Twitter at @ElisaKae.

ALTER EGO IN A RED TIE

LOTIS CERVANTES

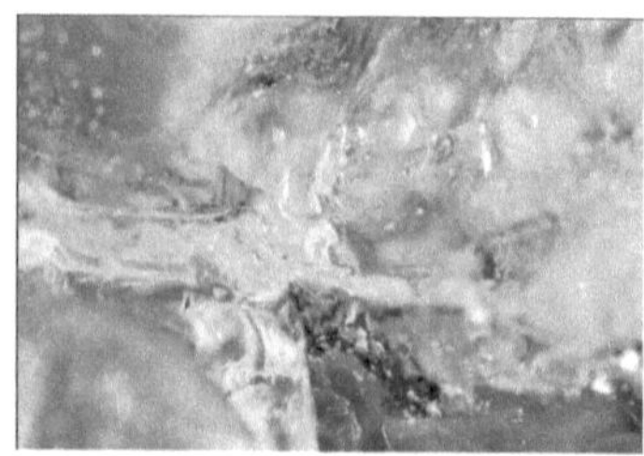

Sara and I were dating for almost two years now and everything had been going really well.

Until two days ago...

'Will you marry me?'

We were celebrating her promotion to manager in the bookstore she worked in since we met, and the question came after my nth orgasm (I lost count).

I felt amazing. And then...

'Will you marry me?'

Suddenly, my mouth went dry and my body felt cold.

The passionate heat escaped my being like a deer running for dear life.

She opened the drawer in the nightstand and took out a small black box but before she could show me what was inside, I untangled myself from her embrace.

I ran to the bathroom where I looked at my pale face in the mirror.

My hazel eyes were green with fear.

'Are you okay?' I heard her voice behind the closed door.

'Yeah,' I lied.

I was not okay.

Why would she even ask that question?

THE VERY FIRST time we met, we were both in a bar, sitting by ourselves, each of us nursing a broken heart.

My fiancé just broke off our engagement because he realized he wasn't ready to settle down.

'I was pressured and it's not fair to you, Nat,' he reasoned.

I asked if it was just his excuse because there was someone else.

There was no one, he insisted.

His two sisters vouched for his words.

They said they were sorry for me.

They confirmed that their domineering mother pushed him to ask the question. He was the only single person in their family. His mother kept reiterating that it was time he asked to marry me—that it was time he 'asked for my hand in marriage,' her exact words—so that he would have someone to take care of him.

Now, when I think of his reason for asking me, I'm glad that we didn't go through with it.

Why should I have to take care of him, of anyone anyway? He was a grown-up.

If he was going to marry me, it should be because he loved me and not because he wanted a caregiver.

But before I got to that realization, I drowned myself in countless shots of tequila.

The bar in which I was drowning myself—or at least my sorrows—was unfamiliar. I was avoiding the places I used to go to with my ex.

I didn't want to cross paths with someone I knew and hear another 'Oh, Nat, we just heard, so sorry.'

I was humiliated enough.

That night, I only wanted to forget my misery.

I was well into my nth shot (I lost count) when a woman with very short hair sat beside me.

My peripheral vision, although slowly turning blurry, was impressed with what I saw.

She was wearing an unbuttoned navy blue suit, cream-coloured shirt, and a red tie.

Bold, I thought to myself.

I drank the tequila I was holding and then had a sudden urge to turn from where I was seated to look around the bar.

I had never seen so many women in one space in my life before.

When I realized where I was, I burst out laughing.

The woman shot me a glance.

I laughed so hard that other people began to look my way.

'Are you okay?' I heard the woman ask while I wiped the tears from my eyes.

'No, I'm not!' I blurted.

Without meaning to, I began to cry.

'Oh...kay,' the woman said to me when I started bawling.

The scene I made attracted attention again. I forced myself into silence, and with tear-soaked eyes, I scanned the room.

Everywhere, happy people. Dancing, kissing. Having fun.

I wanted to run away. Quickly. I stood up and lost my footing before I could make the first step.

The woman in the red tie caught me before I fell and embarrassed myself even more.

But at the time, I didn't quite appreciate that.

'Let... go... of... me,' I slurred.

'I would like to do that but I won't,' she replied. 'Why don't I call you a cab?'

She had one arm around me.

With her body so close to mine, I caught a whiff of her perfume.

She smelled like... linens.

Soft, clean, I-want-to-stay-in-bed-with-you-longer linens.

Even in my alcohol-addled mind, I knew there was no way I would get into bed with this gorgeous woman.

Or so I thought.

❧

I WOKE up the next day in an unfamiliar room wearing nothing but my underwear.

Oh shit!

I got up and tried to remember what I happened the previous night.

The woman!

What the hell did I do? I would later learn that I threw up on my clothes, my shoes and everywhere else.

I moved so fast that the room started spinning.

I held on to the bedpost to steady myself.

Oh Nat!

Alcohol was never your friend.

When are you going to learn?

I sat on the bed and thought of what to do when I heard a gentle knock on the door.

'Are you awake?' The deep and raspy voice was familiar.

'Y... yes,' I answered.

'Can I come in?'

'No!' I yelled.

'Why not?' she countered.

'You know why,' I replied.

'Oh yeah. Why don't you just grab some clothes from the closet? I think we're about the same size.'

Yeah, right. I thought.

I might have been plastered last night but I could tell that she was taller.

She was wearing flats and she still towered over my five foot six frame.

'Are you cool with that?' she spoke again.

'It's cool,' I replied.

'If you don't come out in five minutes, I'm coming in,' she warned.

I stood up and walked to the closet.

There were suits of different colours and fabrics. And a lot of red ties.

I found a pair of blue sweatpants and a gray cotton shirt.

I was right about the height difference—I had to fold up the hem of her pants more than two inches.

But I was dressed and out of the bedroom within my five minute deadline.

The woman was sitting at the dining table, reading a newspaper.

My peripheral vision wasn't lying.

She was gorgeous as hell.

Tall, tan, young, lovely.

Tall and tan, young and lovely.

Tall and tan and young and lovely.

The words played in my mind on a loop, like a sweet, uninvited refrain.

❧

THAT FIRST UNUSUAL meeting led to coffee, then to one dinner and then another and another, until I realized that I was falling in love with Sara.

It was surreal. Not because she was also a woman. But because she got me. She got me so completely.

I admired her quiet strength.

She was the antithesis to my unquenchable fire.

Early on, she told me that the reason she was at the bar that night was because she was mourning her own heartache.

It had been a year since her ex left her for a man.

'I wasn't surprised. She told me she was bi,' Sara explained. 'But when your heart is set on spending your life with one person only to find out that she doesn't ultimately share that goal, it kinda sucks, you know.'

I told her about my ex and the reason why he proposed to me.

'It does suck!' I agreed.

My initial reaction to my evolving feelings for Sara was fear.

I knew who she was but did I know who I was?

Undeniably, since we met, I moved from heartbreak to happiness.

I was still moving on—it was a long process—but having Sara by my side made it easier.

When I cried from the pain of my failed engagement, she was there with a box of Kleenex in hand.

When I was terrified that I would never find someone to love me, she calmed my fear by telling me what was beautiful and good about me.

'It's his loss that he changed his mind,' Sara told me one time.

'Yes, it is, because I'm a very good cook!'

We laughed at the inside joke.

There was something uncomplicated between us.

It was beautiful. And I loved it.

So when I discovered that I wanted more than just friendship from her, I panicked.

I was concerned with losing everything good with us.

My terror-stricken heart decided to do what I thought was best.

I left.

Not just her.

The country.

❧

MY TRIP to Thailand was hot and disconcerting.

I left Canada but carried heavy emotional baggage.

Sara must be furious that I left, I thought, on the way to the plane, on the plane, on the hot Thai tarmac, everywhere I stepped.

I didn't tell her where I was going.

I didn't tell her I was leaving.

During my visits to Thailand's Buddhist temples, I begged the gods for guidance.

Did they give it? On the third day, I knew.

I was in love.

What else did I need to know or to feel?

❧

I SPENT the remaining days of my two-week vacation in peace.

The blues of the ocean were more vibrant.

The sand beneath my feet was warm and comforting.

The trek to the mountains was less daunting.

My heart was joyful and couldn't wait to get back.

I looked forward to seeing Sara.

I held on to this thought till my plane touched down in Canada.

Being missing in action, however, had consequences: Sara wasn't pleased to see me.

'You don't just disappear and assume that when you come back, you'll be welcomed with open arms,' she said to me when I came over to her apartment.

'I know that and I'm sorry,' I said.

She was sitting on the couch across from me, cold and distant.

What could I say? Only one thing.

'I'm in love with you,' I said.

The creases in her forehead deepened and her eyes studied me for a long time.

'What did you say?' Her tone wasn't angry.

'Do I really need to repeat it?'

'I wanted to make sure I heard you right,' she replied.

Instead of saying it, I crossed the space between us and kissed her lips.

She welcomed the move by opening her mouth and deepening the kiss with her tongue.

Before I lost myself in her kiss, I moved away.

'I think you heard what I said,' I teased.

❧

THE BEGINNING of a new love is always wonderful and filled with possibilities.

Sara and I loved each other. Were committed to each other.

But.

'I don't want to get married,' I told her.

'Why not?' Her face didn't show any signs of disappointment, just curiosity. 'Is it because of what happened to you before?'

'I want to marry for the right reasons,' I answered.

'Am I not the right reason?' she countered.

'It's not that, Sara.'

'So what is it then?'

I didn't answer.

I couldn't tell her the truth.

I couldn't bear to admit the humiliation I felt when my engagement was cancelled.

Going through that rejection was a blow to my ego and my identity as a woman.

I questioned my worth.

I blamed myself.

My self-respect was shattered.

Even though I knew, rationally, it wasn't my fault, the damage was done.

There was always the nagging fear that it could happen again.

I wanted to protect myself and to do that, I swore off marriage. Or at least, put it off into the very, very distant future.

'Can we at least revisit it when the time comes?' Sara's smile melted my heart.

'Okay,' I answered.

So now. She did.

❧

I LEANED on the door and listened for sounds from the bedroom.

Sara must have fallen asleep.

I turned the tap on and washed my face.

Sara.

Sara was always a step ahead of me.

There was an empty space in her closet for my clothes for when I spent the night with her.

There were two toothbrushes beside her bathroom sink.

There was a spare key ready for when... if I ever decided to move in with her.

Sara.

There was no doubt that she loved me.

Then why was I so scared to take the next step?

❧

I OPENED the bathroom door and stepped outside.

The night lamp was on and the bed was empty.

There was a post-it note on top of the headboard with the small black box on top of it.

I felt a punch in my gut as I picked up the yellow paper.

Sara's handwriting.

'When you're ready.'

❧

WHEN I CAME BACK from Thailand and Sara was livid that I left without a word, I understood that she was worried but couldn't fully empathize with her.

Now that I couldn't get a hold of her and my calls were going directly to voicemail, I knew how she felt.

Desperate for contact, answers, I went to the bookstore.

'She's in California,' her assistant told me.

'For how long?'

The girl with the thick round glasses eyed me suspiciously.

'Look, we had a misunderstanding and I'm worried.'

'She's flying back tonight, I think.'

'Do you know what time?'

'Around 8-ish?'

I hugged her and left.

❧

I'VE NEVER BEEN one for grand gestures.

Even when my ex proposed, he knew not to hire people for a flash mob.

We were having a quiet dinner and the ring wasn't in the champagne glass or dessert but in the pocket of the coat he was wearing.

Declaring my love for Sara was my boldest act.

Confirming my love... what could I do?

At the airport, I paced the room, nervous.

I checked the flight schedules countless times to make sure that the information I received was legit.

True enough, there was a flight from San Francisco that was arriving at 8:23 p.m.

'On schedule,' the display board assured me.

I sat in the waiting lounge opposite the black and white monitor, watching the flow of people coming in.

My palms were sweaty and my heart was racing.

I wasn't sure of what I'm doing but I knew what I wanted.

What if you're too late? a voice inside my head whispered.

I pushed the thought aside.

It's going to be fine, I said to myself.

I checked my watch.

In fifteen minutes, Sara's plane would be here.

Every second dragged on.

What if she rejected me?

God!

I didn't know how I would take it. Would I survive?

When it happened the first time, I was devastated but it wasn't my fault.

Having someone to blame helped.

If Sara refused, I would only have myself to blame.

She was the right reason.

I looked at the monitor again and saw that the plane from San Francisco had arrived.

I stood up and walked in front of the exit door, quivering with fear and anticipation.

The door opened. One by one, the passengers came out and were greeted by their loved-ones.

No Sara.

What if her flight changed?

The doubts fueled my anxiety.

I stood next to a woman who was also watching the door.

A red-haired bearded man came out and she walked to meet him.

The two of them kissed.

More and more people came. Then fewer. Fewer. A trickle.

My heart pounded and my hope waned.

The door closed and most of the new arrivals were gone.

My shoulders slumped in dismay.

I watched the door, wishing it would open again.

I wished for Sara to appear in front of me.

She didn't.

I turned away.

Voices.

Sara?

I turned around just as Sara came out, the flight crew behind her.

My eyes watered, and my breath stopped.

Just like on the day we met, she was wearing an unbuttoned navy blue suit, cream-coloured shirt, and a red tie.

Hands shaking, I raised the poster I brought with me.

'Nat?' she looked at my face and then at the neon pink poster.

SARA, YOU ARE
ALL THE RIGHT REASONS.
WILL YOU MARRY ME?

The pilots and flight attendants were looking up as well.

A guy I hired to play the song 'I'm yours' was standing beside me with his guitar. I forgot to cue him, but it didn't matter. He was strumming and singing, but neither of us was paying any attention to him.

'Is it a yes?' I asked.

She didn't say a word.

Instead, she walked to where I was standing and drowned me in her kiss.

❧

***Lotis Cervantes** was born in the Philippines and adopted by Canada. You can find some of her work on Wattpad at Wattpad.com/user/LCCervantes.*

ABOUT THE PHOTOGRAPHER

JENNIFER WEIHMANN

The photographs illustrating *Screw Chocolate 2*, including the components of the mosaic in the cover image, are all the work of Jennifer Weihmann. To view them in a more aesthetically appropriate size and to appreciate their glorious colour palette, visit the multimedia edition of *Screw Chocolate (1&2)* at *mjanecolette.com/ScrewChocolate* or Jennifer Weihmann's Instagram at *@jweihmann.photo.*

❧

Jennifer Weihmann*'s art photography is her passion. Jennifer's formal studies were in Communications, Visual Studies, and Art History at the University of Calgary. She's had several solo and group exhibitions, and in February 2018, she will be a featured emerging artist at* Exposure, *Alberta's photography festival. Jennifer is known as a landscape photographer, but she also has a body of work documenting the lives of a group of adults, with whom she embedded herself, living on the streets of Texas. She also photographs musicians—portraits and during rehearsals.*

Since moving to Calgary in 2003, she has concentrated on the natural environment surrounding her adopted city.

Jennifer's relationship with the natural world is organic, visceral and raw—exploiting nature's perfect metaphors! The colourful, organic environmental objects she works with, and the challenge of photographing this material, present innumerable opportunities for visual metaphors that express the intricate and delicate nature of our lives.

If you wish to explore more of Jennifer's work, please follow her on Instagram at @jweihmann.photo or visit her website at jenniferweihmannphotography.ca.

ABOUT YYC QUEER WRITERS

SCREW CHOCOLATE: *14 Queer Valentines To Help You Survive February 14* is the first collaborative project by YYC Queer Writers, formed in 2013 by writer and activist Dallas Barnes. We get together intermittently to… write. Also, laud our lovers. Commiserate about our exes. Share what we wrote. Explain what we want to write. Try to justify why we aren't writing it. Go home and write it. Come back. Share it… repeat.

You can read our valentines on-line, see Jennifer Weihmann's fabulous photography in full colour, and listen to some of them too, at *mjanecolette.com/ScrewChocolate.*

❧

In YYC and want to write with us? Find us on Facebook at Calgary Queer Writing Group or visit *mjanecolette.com/yycqueerwriters* for contact details.

www.ingramcontent.com/pod-product-compliance
Lightning Source LLC
Chambersburg PA
CBHW050158110726
47898CB00008B/2855

* 9 7 8 1 7 7 5 1 8 0 9 0 6 *